Whispers Of My World

Aditi Reddy Vinnamala

BookLeaf
Publishing

India | USA | UK

Made with ❤ on the BookLeaf Publishing Platform
www.bookleafpub.in
www.bookleafpub.com

Dedication

Now, there are many people I would like to thank... and I have later in the book.

However these two people have helped me become the person I am today.

My Mom of-course; but also my english teacher who changed my perspective on English, not only as a subject but as a language. If my 2024 january self knew that shed be writing a book at the begining of 2025, her jaw would have dropped way beneath the earths core!

So here's to:

My mom - your love has been the light that guides me through everything. Thank you for believing in me even when I doubted myself, for cheering me on through every poem, and for teaching me that my words have power. This book exists because you never let me give up.

Monalisha Ma'am (My English Teacher) - Thank you for nurturing my voice, for your gentle guidance, and for showing me the beauty in every verse. Your encouragement turned my scattered thoughts into poetry, and your belief in me helped shape every page of this book.

Preface

Dear Readers,

Hi! I'm Aditi — a simple eighth grader with a not-so-simple imagination. I was given a wonderful opportunity to write this book, and what a journey it has been! *Whispers of My World* is a collection of 21 poems that reflect how I see the world around me — and the world within me. Through these poems, I've explored everything from the quiet struggles of a woman's life to the playful battles between my socks and shoes. Yes, you read that right!

Writing this book hasn't just been about putting words on paper. It's been about opening a door into the corners of my mind I didn't even know existed. It's been a journey of self-discovery, wonder, and imagination.

Each poem in this book holds a piece of me — a thought, a feeling, a spark. Every one of them is unique, with its own voice, its own message, and its own little world.

I hope that as you turn the pages, you'll laugh, wonder, reflect, and maybe even see things a little differently — just like I did while writing them.

Thank you for holding a piece of my world in your hands.

Welcome to *Whispers of My World.*

With all my heart,
Aditi

Acknowledgements

Whispers of My World is more than just a collection of poems - it's a piece of my heart, shaped and supported by the people around me.

To my English teacher, thank you for helping me shape these poems into their best form. Your guidance, encouragement, and belief in my writing gave me the confidence to keep going.

To my parents, your endless support and motivation kept me focused, even on the days I wanted to give up. Thank you for reminding me of the magic I hold within me.

To my friends, thank you for clapping after every poem I shared, for cheering me on, and for never getting tired of my constant "yapping" about writing a book. Your enthusiasm made the journey even more special.

And to one very special person - the kid who helped me through middle school - thank you. So many of the memories we shared have quietly found their way into these poems. This book holds fragments of those moments, and I'm grateful for every one of them.

Lastly, a big thank you to ChatGPT - for helping me find rhymes for words I thought were unrhymable, and for fixing my spellings (which was *extremely* necessary...serioulsy).

P.S. I did write all the poems myself - promise!

Everyone should be allowed to have a little AI magic on their side.

To everyone who stood by me, listened, encouraged, and believed — this book is as much yours as it is mine.

With all my heart,

Aditi

1. Her Silent Storm

She wakes up and fights
For every one of her rights,
And sometimes she cries
Only to be criticised.

She's in pain every month,
Which lasts for a while
But when she bears a child,
It brings her an endless smile.

Her life is like a storm
Isn't it such a shame,
The same women that give us life
Have no rights to their name.

Every street that she walks by
Turns a naked eye
Despite all the burdens she carries,
She never asks for any brownies.

These are a woman's struggles
And this is all what she juggles.

Although it is rough
Every woman is tough
Taking every challenge in their stride,
They still walk home with pride.

2. Yet. Both Emotions

A smile
Something that makes you laugh
A cry something that makes you sad
Yet. Both emotions
And emotions you face

A laugh
Something that makes you tickle
A sad
Something that makes you blue
Yet. Both emotions
And emotions you face

A joy
Something that makes you fly
A anger
Something that makes you fight
Yet. Both emotions
And emotions you face

It may not make sense
And it will make you tense
Yet. All emotions
And emotions you face

(A poem inspired by "People Equal" - James Berry)

3. Fearless And Free

When thunder pours, a child screams
When lighting strikes, a child gleams
When the wind whistles, a child dreams
When rain fills the park, a child complains

If the sun's out, a child plays
If a snowflakes fall, a child stays
If silence lingers, a child makes noise
If a crowd gathers, a child finds poise

These small hands, hold worlds untold,
As their hearts run wild and their minds turn bold
Too clever , too free for the rules we make
Too bright for the walls adults forsake

So if the world ever stops spinning
And if time slows down and fades to past
Just know the children will still remain-
Laughing, wondering and dancing in the rain.

4. A View Like No Other

As the sun plays hide and seek,
I step outside for a peek.
children laugh and run below,
While birds drift with the evening glow.
This is my balcony
My favourite place to solace

The wind whispers of against my skin,
The sky glows with this purple colour.
This is my balcony
And it surely is like no other

The most beautiful place i've seen
So peaceful, so serene
This is my balcony.
My favourite place to be!

"A Poem Dedicated To My Dad "

5. Just Us Girls

There's always the scary one,
But she's the boldest and the brightest.
There's always the funny one,
With a laugh that's the strongest.

There's always the shy one,
But her heart is always the kindest.
There's always the loud one,
From inside she's the wildest.

This is my friend group -
A mix of moods and flavours
A rainbow painted boldly
In all are different colours
Were a roller coaster of feelings
With thoughts that touch the ceilings

But at the end of the day...

Were just a group of girls,

Doing what we must.
With love, with laughter,
And unbreakable trust.

6. Whispers of My World

When I step into my world
Memories dance upon the wall,
As my dresser stands tall.

When I step into my world
My bright pink bed comes to sight,
Yet I've barely slept there a night.

When I step into my world
My morning perfume fills the air,
Delicate like petals, light and rare.

When I step into my world
I feel candy dreams and midnight stairs,
Sweetness lingers everywhere.

My world is my space
My space where I am free,
My space where I am - nothing but me.

7. Bestie Energy, Always

When She's by my side
It just feels so right
When I want to cry
She makes me fight

She laughs at every joke
Even if they make her choke
She's always their
To listen , to love , to care

She's the reason I thrive
The best soul alive
And if she ever says goodbye,
I know i'd break inside.

Her lively spirit
Makes me jump like a cricket,
And all of her moves
Can make anyone groove.

This is a poem
To my ride or die
I'll give you a hint...
We wrote a song that touches the sky.

Every bus ride home with you
Is so perfect , so true
I know im leaving this school
But i'll never forget you...

8. The Hearts I Want To Mirror

My mom
The one who lifts me when I fall
And remind me to always stand tall
The one who pushes me to fly
With her bright spirit soaring high
The most perfect soul alive
At least through my eyes

My dad
The one who cheers me when i'm low
And makes me feel free wherever I go
The one who makes me cringe and laugh
But he's the best - my better half
The one who takes me out on walks
Where silence breaks with are heart - to - heart talks

These are the most perfect people I know,
With every challenge they face
They handle it with strength and grace

These are my parents -
my biggest pride
And the kind of people
I want to be inside

9. Nature's Clock

When the clock turns to spring,
The final school bells ring.
Kids leap high with glee,
Running wild and free.

When the clock turns to summer,
Children dive into the pool.
Laughter echoes through the heat,
In the sun, they stay cool.

When the clock turns to autumn,
Jackets begin to appear.
Leaves drift down like golden rain,
And the breeze grows crisp and clear.

When the clock turns to winter,
Snowflakes softly spin around.
The world wears a coat of white,
With silence blanketing the ground.

10. When The Future Comes

When the future comes,
I want to grow.
I want to be
A dancing crow.

I want to see the whole world glow,
Lit by powers I'll come to know.
I want to shine - superstar,
To dream out loud and reach the stars.

I want a child of my own someday,
To take to the park and watch them play.
I want a car that's bold and rare -
Something green, with a wild flair.

I want to go, to Harvard one day,
To learn, to lead, to find my way.
To walk through halls where legends stood,
And shape the world the best I could.

I want to grow with grace and glee,
With a heart that's light, and a spirit free.

This is a poem to my future self,
And I hope I don't end up stuck on a shelf.
I want my wishes to all come true—
Through effort and grit in all that I do.

11. This Is Anxiety

When I speak,
I feel weak.
But when I'm alone,
That's when I peak.
This is anxiety—
It tries to silence me.

When I'm busy,
I barely notice.
But when I pause,
It starts to focus.
This is anxiety—
And I just want to break free.

Every time my stomach churns,
Every corner my vision turns,
Every second I feel so small,
Every moment I fear I'll fall.

This is anxiety.

It tries to swallow me.
But this is anxiety,
And I want it off of me.

12. Magic In The Storm

When the clouds make their grand entrance,
The sun quietly says goodbye.
The rain holds its breath,
Then the sky begins to cry.

Lightning flashes a crooked "hi,"
While thunder shouts its name.
The trees bow low beneath the wind,
And nothing feels the same.

Puddles bloom across the street,
Footsteps vanish in their trail.
The rooftops drum a rhythmic beat,
As the winds begin to wail.

The birds retreat, the flowers close,
The world turns pale and gray.
But still, there's magic in the storm
That never fades away.

13. With Love, The Sunset.

Dear Sky,

With every stroke of colour,
I painted you with wonder.
Every cloud of yours
Held a splash of mine.
But now, it's time -
It's time to say goodbye.

Soon I'll return,
Return with the dawn.
But for now, I'll leave the moon,
The moon as my pawn.

I'll scatter a few stars,
And I'll send Mars -
These will be your gifts
For tonight's gentle drifts.

So this is goodnight,

I'll be back when it's bright.

With love,
The Sunset

14. Forever In These Halls

My school is more than bricks and walls,
It's a place where every spirit stands tall.
A place where students laugh and grow,
With dreams that bloom and friendships flow.

Each hallway whispers tales of old,
Of secrets shared and memories gold.
The library where dreams took flight,
And classes that lit my mind so bright.

When the lunch bell rings, we rush inside,
Where joy and chatter never hide.
The lunch hall buzzes - a daily parade,
Of trays and tales and laughter replayed.

Though time moves on and we must part,
These memories live within my heart.
For one thing's clear and always true -
My school shaped the best in me and you.

15. When Time Froze

The clock stopped ticking,
And the sun stopped moving.
The world was high and bright,
But the birds and leaves froze tight.
Everything slipped into a pause
Shadows stood still on the walls,
Yet no one noticed time at all.

The people carried on
Laughing, working, walking
And they all seemed
So blind to the strange.

I could see everything,
But I felt so alone,
Like all the people near me
Were living beneath a stone.
Was it time that froze,
Or the people who chose
To move without truly seeing,

To live without truly being?

Maybe time stops when hearts grow cold,
When stories stay quiet and dreams grow old.
Maybe the stillness isn't the end
But a silent plea for the world to mend.

16. Grateful For The Small

Each morning arrives with whispers,
I slip into soft old slippers.
The sky begins to hush,
As the world begins to rush.

I smell the beauty of the trees,
And chuckle at her laugh - so free.
I savour honey from the bees,
And take in every tiny beat.

All the messages I send,
Are pieces of me I gently lend
A joke, a thought, a midnight sigh,
A little "hello" just drifting by.

The world's a harsh and hurried place,
Where everything's just one big race.
So I'll take a breath, let the moment stay,
And feel my thanks in a quiet array.

With all its chaos, joy, and sham,
I realise how grateful I am.

17. "Always and Forever"

He was my first secret keeper,
My partner in quiet crimes,
A hand that held my childhood
Through all its clumsy times.

He was the one who stood by me,
The one who inspired me,
The one who cried with me,
And the one who'd fight with me.

Our endless love,
Hidden between the scars,
The scars we gave each other,
Fighting over mars.

He's my biggest cheerleader,
A silent risk-taker.
But at the end of the day,
He's my one and only brother.

Our bond is strong
As steady as a river.
We're there for each other,
"Always and Forever"

18. Silence At Its Peak

In the hush of twilight
Theres a sound so bright
Beneath the unspoken words,
lie stories left unheard.

In the darkness of nature
There's a voice so serene
So sweet and clean,
Yet dangerously mean.

Its powerful and strong,
It makes you feel wrong
Like shadows dancing is the dusk,
Silence settles, thick as dust.

It wraps around you
Like it's the last truth.
The quietest sound
That still speaks the most.

A thousand thoughts left unvoiced
Leaving us with no choice
Between us, an eternal pause speaks,
This pause is silence at its peak...

19. The Endless Battle

I lay on the floor, tired and bent,
Stuffed in the dark wherever I'm sent.
"My threads are worn!" the sock complained.
"You're nothing without me," the shoe explained.

My stripes and colours - all faded past,
By a stink that seems destined to last.
"All because of you," the sock accused,
"You walk the world, I'm just abused!"

"You'll always be hidden," the shoe murmured low,
"I carry the weight - you just tag along slow."
"I'll make you forbidden!" the sock sharply raged,
Their decades of bickering once more engaged.

This battle's eternal, neither side won,
From sunrise to moonlight - it's never done.
In dusty closets or under school pews,
Burns the endless fury...
Between the socks and the shoes.

20. The Girl Who Spoke In Colour

If the world was a colour -
it would be like no other.
But there is a girl
who speaks with these colours.

Every word that she says
leaves one confused, curious, and cold.
But she means something better -
The others are just old.

With every red, she screams,
shows all her fiery dreams.
With every purple, she gleams,
reveals her serene themes.

Her life is like a rainbow -
every colour speaks a language.
She's like a magical scarecrow,
Yet no one seems to understand this.

She's trapped in a world,
A world like no other -
A world with a colour
That smells just like her mother.

21. Facing the Storm

It starts with a word that stiffens the air,
A diagnosis that stings, leaving you in despair.
Tears drip down as you tell your loved ones,
It feels like your world has ended, and it's all undone.

But you push, and you try,
Stay strong, even when you want to cry.
You stand tall through each injection,
Fighting on with quiet determination.

Every tablet you take,
Is a step in the journey you make.
With every treatment, though it's tough,
You find the strength to rise above.

Though it's rough,
You remain tough.
Each journey is different,
But you walk away with a smile, resilient and brilliant.

(Dedicated to my 6 year old cousin, who battled his way out!)

35